MW01075345

Doing Hypnosis:

Professional Instruction Manual Series

Edward F. Mackey, PhD

Contents

Introduction

There is a plethora of material written on hypnosis. Much recounts the similar history and background of hypnosis, its emergence and submergence several times throughout history and its recent accounts since the time of Mesmer. You can read about the many luminaries of hypnosis discussing their particular theory about trance, the particular scaling they developed to identify if and when a particular subject is in trance and of course you can read the voluminous definitions of hypnosis that have been proposed throughout history. It is interesting to note that even today it is difficult to find professionals using hypnosis to agree on just what trance is, when it begins and ends, who should be doing hypnosis and who should not! This amounts to a great deal of misunderstanding from a professional standpoint, let alone the understanding from a patient perspective. It is no wonder there are so many misunderstandings and misconceptions from the public sector.

It is important for everyone to realize that trance occurs, much the same as sleep occurs. It is a natural and everyday occurrence. Trance can develop at certain times and under certain circumstances. Trance can and does develop spontaneously and at other times can be deliberately obtained. There are professionals that believe trance is non-therapeutic on its own. This is akin to believing sleep is non-therapeutic. Once an individual experiences deliberate trance induction, the realization of its efficacy becomes glaringly apparent. Once an individual experiences a wonderful night's sleep, the realization of sleep's efficacy is glaringly apparent. This does not imply that trance is sleep, trance stands on its own.

This text will move in a different direction than the aforementioned material. It is designed to provide direction and concrete examples to the professional desiring to understand suggestive therapeutics and to utilize the power of hypnotic trance in their practice. One important caveat to the understanding and use of trance is: It is essential that the professional utilize trance in their own lives. Self-trancework is so important and cannot be overemphasized enough. It is simple fact that no one can take or lead another to someplace they have not been themselves. Once you have been to and experienced deliberate trance you become much more convincing to the patient. Subconscious communication occurs constantly and the patient will perceive your personal belief at some unconscious level thus increasing effectiveness.

I will begin this instruction with instructions on using language and language style. Then I will be moving on to various types of suggestions and the peculiarities in delivery. This by no means, will attempt to identify all possibilities, as those possibilities are, in fact, limitless! Later in this text I will give some examples that can be used by the practitioner as is, or can be modified using the techniques contained herein.

Getting Started Doing Hypnosis

Beginning to use hypnosis in practice can be daunting to many practitioners. It is understood that, some form of professional education or training has been accomplished prior to using formalized hypnotherapeutic work.

Once this education is accomplished then it is only a matter of how to put formalized hypnosis into play in your practice. This text is the first in a series of publications designed to help you, the practitioner, put hypnotic therapy into your professional practice. It is designed to enhance your understanding of what hypnosis is, how it works and how to incorporate it into a daily regimen.

Practice, practice, practice, and more practice! This is a crucial key into becoming familiar and comfortable with hypnotic techniques. It is also very crucial to be using hypnosis in your own life. Using self-hypnosis on a daily basis, positive self-talk and positive self-suggestion every day, goes a long way into becoming very comfortable with trance work. It is very important that you know what trance is and what trance feels like, which leads to a belief in using trance powerfully! The works of George Estabrooks, a contemporary of Erickson, suggested that, "...the client will not actualize what the therapist does not believe". (Estabrooks, p. 110, *Hypnotism*). This truth is very clear. When you consider that you are attempting to lead a patient/client into trance and effect positive outcomes, this begs the question: How can you effectively lead anyone somewhere that you have not gone before? Self-hypnotic work is perhaps the most important practice that you, the practitioner, must do in order to become effective.

Once you begin to see, feel and experience positive change in your own life it seemingly becomes effortless to assist others in doing so as well. Think about this for a moment: Unconscious chemical communication in the form of neuropeptides is occurring continuously (Pert, 1997). These neuropeptides originally thought to be located only in the central nervous system are now found throughout our entire body (Pert, 1997, Brown, P., 1991, Overdurf & Silverthorn, 1994). All things in the body and mind are communicating with everything else and it is happening automatically and unconsciously. Whatever you believe yourself to be, please understand now, that you are much more than that! Imagine now, what that statement can mean to your patient/client when you exude that belief at a conscious and unconscious level!

It Starts with Communication

As professionals, we influence patient care and outcomes in a powerful way. Health care professionals interaction with various types of patients, accounts for a large percentage of direct patient contact (Kozier, Erb, Berman & Snyder, 2004). Patients respond to authority figures in a variety of ways (Comer, 2001; Crist, Armer & Radina, 2002) and these responses can be both positive and negative in nature (Comer, 2001; Santrock, 2006). Positive responders look toward the practitioner as an authority figure and this can move patient interaction in a positive therapeutic direction. The proper use of words, suggestion, inflection and proper attitude go a long way to enhance patient therapeutic outcomes no matter what the setting or where the patient interaction takes place (Battino, 2007; Brown & Draper, 2003; Holden 1988; Mackey, 2009; Mackey 2010).

Language communicates our beliefs, attitudes, expectations and feelings to those with whom we are communicating. Positive words may uplift and heal while negative words may harm and have an opposite effect (White, 2005). Dr. Ray Birdwhistle was an American anthropologist who studied nonverbal communication among other things. Birdwhistle is perhaps most famous for suggesting that communication is made up of 7% words, 38% tonality and 55% non-verbal cues (Meharabian & Ferris, 1967). Birdwhistle pointed out that human gestures differed from other animals in that human gesturing is polysemic, meaning they can be interpreted in many different ways depending upon the context in which they are utilized, and he resisted the notion that body language could be interpreted in an absolute fashion (Birdwhistle, 1970). It can be understood from the work of Birdwhistle, that words themselves contribute only a small percentage of the conveyed meaning to the receiver. The tones in which the words are delivered and the manner in which words are delivered carry a much greater portion of the conveyed meaning. These concepts are incredibly important to the health care provider who is a most personal caregiver to the patient within the context of a professional/patient role (Birdwhistle, 1970; Brown & Draper, 2003; Mehrabian & Ferris, 1967: Roykulcharoen & Good, 2004).

Suggestion as part of communication occurs continuously (Hilgarde, 1965; Hilgarde & Hilgarde, 1994; Kane & Olness, 2004; Mackey 2010; Voit & Delaney, 2004; Yapko, 2003), understanding this fact can assist the professional in delivering positive suggestion to enhance the patient outcome whatever the therapeutic environment (Kane & Olness, 2004; Mackey 2009; Mackey 2010; Roykulcharoen & Good, 2004). The knowledge of these concepts is invaluable to health care professionals (HCP) as they interact with patients. When a professional sends mixed signals, i.e. their non-verbal cues or tonality does not match up with the words used, incongruent communication occurs and impacts how the message is received. It is of the utmost importance for the HCP to recognize their demeanor and attitude convey much more than the words used during conversation. Irony, approval, scorn, humor, sarcasm and other perceptions are suggested by how something is said rather than the actual words use (Holden, 1988; Kane & Olness, 2004). The most interesting thing is how humans convey messages within messages at an unconscious level. Indeed, we are not aware of how we ourselves respond and signal to others at an unconscious or subconscious level (Bandler, 2008; Kane & Olness, 2004; Overdurf & Silverthorn, 1994). These subconscious perceptions influence not only how we ourselves feel and behave but affect the patients we care for profoundly at an unconscious level.

What to Do

Once the previous information about language and

communication is understood by the health care provider, it is easy to incorporate certain techniques and style into the therapeutic patient interaction. From the Birdwhistle study, it is seen that the manner in which one carries oneself (posture, dress, etc.) lends a large percentage (55%) to the meanings of any communication. In other words, be professional in your mannerisms and address patients professionally and courteously. The patient looks toward the professional as an authority and the words and communications from an authority weigh in on the conscious and subconscious mind of the patient (Kane & Olness, 2004; White, 2004). Using appropriate tone when speaking provides up to 38% of the meaning the patient receives from any message (Meharabian, 1967). The words used in the communication should be appropriate and used effectively as well. For example, it is preferred to use the word "comfort" over the word "pain" as positron emission tomography (PET) scans and functional magnetic resonance imaging (fMRI) scans have identified different areas of the brain are engaged when using different words (Jensen, 2011). Of course there are times when the practitioner may be unable to avoid using certain words, i.e. with a "pain" scale, but remember the tonality and the non-verbal cues given at the same time carry much of the inferred meaning to a patient (Birdwhistle, 1970; Mackey 2010; Mehrabian, 1967; White, 2004).

One method to assisting the early practitioner to develop style, intonation and a smooth patter is to audiotape themselves. Using a recorder will identify areas needing improvement and to develop a confidence in the wording of suggestion and its delivery. The advantage here is that one can go over and over the material until it becomes second nature, much like a professional athlete will practice their sport thousands of times until muscle memory takes over. Learning to incorporate the strategies, both verbal and non-verbal, will increase efficacy in therapeutic outcomes.

Building Rapport with Patients/Clients

How do you Build Rapport?

Here is a basic rule: *People (patients/clients) like people who are similar to themselves!*

When you demonstrate or show another individual that you are like them in some way, it allows the other person to feel comfortable and safe when around you. When they are comfortable and safe they are much more likely to communicate and share ideas, concerns, problems, etc.

Matching and Mirroring:

This means that in some way the practitioner will copy the behavior of the patient/client. The individual practitioner will mimic the physical gestures or perhaps the tilt of the head, a smile, hand gestures and more. This mimicking behavior sends a message to the client that is perceived at a subconscious level. The message is: **I understand and we are very much alike!**

Problems with matching and mirroring behavior occur when the client realizes at a conscious level that you are mirroring their behavior. The mirroring is then perceived as a form of ridicule or you are making fun of the individual. It is of the utmost importance to have the mirroring and matching behavior remain out of conscious perception!

Mistakes in Rapport Building

Being too nice: Acting out of the ordinary. In other words, most of our interpersonal interaction is matter of fact and not usually too polite or too proper. When these too proper events occur it sends up a red flag to our subconscious that tends to make us more consciously aware of what is happening. When we become too nice sometimes we do it at the expense of real communication and breakdown of rapport occurs.

Trying too hard to establish rapport: This can lead to unconscious signaling that you are desperate to connect with that individual. Think about this for a moment. How many times in your life have you noticed when someone is trying too hard to connect with you? You begin to feel overwhelmed or smothered, get uncomfortable and begin looking for an excuse to bail out. It is important for the practitioner to recall the Law of Reversed Effect: The harder you try to do something the more elusive it becomes!

Lack of real interest in the patient/client: It is amazing to me the number of practitioners that seemingly have no real interest in their patients or clients. These individuals are simply going through the motions. Disregard for another human being is perhaps one of the most easily understood unconscious perceptions. The subconscious mind sends out the signals to the patient/ client that you are disinterested. These perceptions do not lead to rapport building!

It is much easier to establish rapport with your client when you have their best interest at heart. The patient can perceive your intent at an unconscious level and they will again begin to feel safe and comfortable in their interactions with you.

Language reflection is one method to help show genuine interest in your patient. Language reflection is the repetition of exact words the client is using. An example: "I was in the waiting room and I was feeling a bit nervous". You would reflect back to the patient: "So you were in the waiting room and feeling a bit nervous".

Role ambiguity in the therapist/client relationship: The problem here is one of role-play. The role status (that of therapist/client) is one usually regarded as higher/lower. This does not mean that a client is of a lower class only in the particular confines of therapy, is the patient in a lower status.

It is important for the therapist to decide if the therapeutic relationship is one needing to maintain the authoritarian higher status or can it become a more mutually respective one- on- one. In either case, the therapist should maintain professionalism.

How to Establish Rapport

In any case, rapport is crucial to the development of an effective therapeutic relationship. From the aforementioned information you can begin to understand that this relationship forms from the interaction between two people.

A very effective method to establishing rapport is to give your undivided attention to the person in front of you. Put your personal baggage aside, take a moment to compose yourself, then focus on the patient and constantly envision a positive outcome. See the individual in front of you as a wonderful, complete human being, enjoying life to the fullest.

Incorporating Hypnosis in Practice

Definition

So many definitions of hypnosis over centuries have led to much confusion. Theory, conjecture and anecdotal experience have added to the many definitions of the hypnotic trance. A simple and elegant method to understand hypnotic trance is to understand the fact that the subconscious mind is active 24 hours, a day 7 days a week. The conscious mind on the other hand is active only when awake! It is evident then that trance is ongoing and the only variable is the level of conscious awareness or interference. Whether or not all people can be hypnotized has been bantered about by academicians for years, insisting that hypnotizability is a steady trait in society. This is true when one realizes that to test hypnotizability you must set a certain context. Hypnotizability studies are performed within a certain well- defined parameter of suggestion and style (context). The result is then codified by the administrator as to how well someone reacted to that set of parameters. Within that context (whatever that may be) the result is fairly steady, change the context and the result is different, just as Birdwhistle discovered with human gesturing. In other words, if you decide one can dance by whether or not a person is able to do the foxtrot, chicken dance and a waltz and only those within a certain time constraint (right now), then you will eliminate a percentage of the population by default. That does not mean they cannot dance, it simply means they cannot do those particular dances right now in the particular fashion you desire within a certain time constraint for your study.

Hypnosis is contextual and it is imperative for therapeutic intervention that the context be congruent. One method of doing that is to make sure the language used is understood by both sender and receiver. Using language, style, projection, words and combining them all into a suggestion is the beginnings of ensuring the correct context for effectual interaction. This manual will give you a solid foundation to begin those learnings.

Suggestion

Using suggestion in practice is a wonderful tool to accomplish patient goals, care and recovery. It is important to learn the techniques of crafting suggestion, delivering suggestion and utilizing hypnotic principles leading to the hypnotic state deliberately. The hypnotic state is operating continuously; you are simply unaware as the trance state is "unconscious". It is imperative to understand that hypnosis, per se, is suggestion driven. In other words, a person responds to suggestion. This happens continuously as we are being bombarded by suggestion continuously. We receive suggestion via our nervous system from the peripheral nervous system (PNS) as well as from within, via the central nervous system (CNS). Advertising takes advantage of these facts and spends a great deal of money on each ad, making sure it suggests the product as: essential, sexy, enhancing, needed, mandatory, alluring, etc. The suggestions used appeal to our senses and also to our internal framework as jingles, songs, and catchy phrases that we will repeat to ourselves as "self-talk".

Delivering Suggestion through Words, Language and Style

Words have meaning. Words have meaning not only to those speaking the words but to the listener as well. Those meanings may not be the "dictionary definition" but may be an amalgam of what they have learned, read, heard and felt throughout their respective lifetime. It is imperative that we as practitioners understand that meaning is not in the word itself but in the reception and understanding of the listener.

When talking with another individual, especially in a health care setting, practitioners need to be sure to use the right words. These right words are ones that convey the message of the practitioner to the patient/ client. **IF** there is a discrepancy in the translation then a miscommunication will occur. Therefore it is paramount that both the practitioner and the client/patient have an understanding of the words used and the meanings behind them.

How does that happen?

When first meeting the patient/ client, during the intake session, or during the history and physical, much pertinent information can be gleaned. This information intake requires an adept practitioner experienced in the art of communication, talking and rapport. This is the period when tensions can be released, expectations uncovered, meaning established and misconceptions clarified.

It is important to take time with each patient. These few extra minutes of time enables the client or patient to see, feel and understand that you are interested in them uniquely. Doing this increases the rapport developed between patient and practitioner enabling a more robust interaction and better outcomes.

During your first interview with the patient, get an understanding of their style of talking, listening and body language. Take notes and refer to them when treatment planning begins. Using the patient's own language can ensure they will have a better understanding of the material being presented.

Once you have an understanding of their language style and have begun developing rapport effective suggestion delivery occurs easily.

Body Language

Non-verbal cues account for approximately 55% of communication, tonality about 38% and words themselves only 7%. It appears that attentiveness, rapport, sincerity and understanding play a most important role in effective communication and suggestion delivery. If a practitioner seems aloof, disinterested or non-attentive, then they lose a great percentage of effectiveness. If, on the other hand, a practitioner pays attention to detail, developing rapport and showing genuine interest in the patient, the patient/client picks this up in an unconscious way and efficacy increases. Couple this with effective style and delivery and using the right words for a particular client/patient and in the right context, hypnotic work seems effortless.

Speaking

Tonality and pacing of speech is extremely important when delivering suggestion. When speaking to your patient/client and you desire to gain compliance, use a downward inflection. This downward inflection: "Please...sit down now"! is perceived as a command and many times followed immediately without any hesitation as it has bypassed conscious discernment. If the same sentence was spoken as an interrogatory (question): "Please...sit down now"? It leaves room for conscious interpretation of meaning. Using the downward inflection (command style) of suggestion delivery gains much more compliance.

When using suggestion like the above example, you

can begin to expand on the suggestions and build them into a conversational technique that many times becomes very effective. "Please ....sit down....now..................you can begin to notice.......how......good you feel..." You can begin to see when spoken like this, in this manner, downward inflection and the use of appropriate pauses make the conversation take on a very directive, yet, non-intimidating manner.

Attending to your patient/client with positive intent, good posture and eye contact makes communication much more effective. The patient/client can sense that you are vested in their well-being. When you begin the entire process of using hypnosis/suggestion in your practice, please begin with definite good intention. Know that the work you are doing is effective and that the suggestions you are using will bring relief, comfort, etc. The subconscious mind of your patient can pick up your intent in ways we cannot yet understand. It is also essential that you begin to do your own self-suggestion/self-hypnotic work on a daily basis. This self-work enhances you as an individual and also sends the positive message at an unconscious level, to your patient, that following these suggestions will get them to a better place.

Hypnotic Suggestion Delivery

The exercise below demonstrates the use of ambiguity, embedded commands, direct and indirect suggestions.

1) "So it is OK to... *relax now*...or in a minute....it doesn't really matter...."

   When you say "relax now" use downward inflection to give the embedded command to relax. You are also using a pause each time you see the ....
   The entire sentence tells the patient that it is OK to relax, right now...

2) "When you....*go into trance....*"

   This is essentially a command, embedded into the sentence. "Go into trance" is spoken with a downward inflection.

3) "It can, you know… be *easy*…. *To…… let go now…*"

Your patient/client hears and understands that "Yes it can" be "easy" and to "let go now" rather than later!

4) "To let …*your unconscious*….mind help you"

This is another style of command infused into the sentence. "Your unconscious…" infers they are already there! The subconscious takes all literally and will fulfill this if not already happening.

5) *"Resolve your issues now"*

Another command suggestion telling the unconscious mind to "resolve issues now" not later.

6) "So….as you *drift and relax"*

The italicized words are spoken in downward

inflection command style.

7) "You may be aware of sensations in your body....as you ....*Relax more.*"

Another embedded command.

8) "You know....a person is able to...*develop an internal focus of attention*"

The above infers that a person can know something. Which person? Themselves of course. Then an embedded command to develop internal focus (go inside).

9) "And just... *feel good* about themselves...."

A direct command to feel good.

10) "And...eventually *that* troublesome *issue* will just *disappear*.

By emphasizing the italicized words in some manner, they form a command structure. "That issue... will ...disappear."

11) "Isn't it nice to know (now)"

This word "know" can be spoken in a manner that sounds like "now," a time command. This can then be integrated into another sentence.

12) "You can...*integrate these learnings*"

Another command embedded in the conversation when spoken with a downward inflection of the voice.

13) "Whenever...*your unconscious*...is ready"

> Here is another example of a statement about the hypnotic state that can be interpreted as a command that one is already "unconscious or in trance or asleep."

14) "It is enjoyable to *learn something new*...isn't it"?

> An embedded command: "Learn something new", Implies to the listener the instruction to learn.

15) "A person might...you know...*get a whole new perspective*"

> Implies that a person (they) may get that new perspective. Spoken with a pause and then downward inflection of the voice to command: "get a whole new perspective".

34

16) "When you allow *your unconscious*...generate new solutions".

Another statement that the listener is "unconscious".

17) "I wonder if you have already *start to notice.........changes taking place...*".

An ambiguity: You sound like you say "started" but really say "start", as a command. This leads to a short pause and then another command to complete the sentence "start to notice changes taking place".

18) "When you really begin to... *make these patterns a part of your life...*".

A direct suggestion to do something.

19) "Then...you'll feel *freeeee yourself to change*"

Here you will extend the word free a millisecond or two. This sounds to the listener as you are saying "Then you will feel free". As you continue the word free into the sentence it becomes "Free yourself to change", spoken as a command. A type of ambiguity.

20) "By the time you.....*Notice how far you have come......*".

Direct suggestion when spoken in command tone.

21) "You can be excited about the positive change in your life".

Here you can speak this sentence as is or emphasis can be placed on different words to enhance different commands or meanings. Example: "*You* can be excited......about the ....positive .... *change*...in ..*your life*". The words italicized then are emphasized slightly when spoken and become a command to "YOU, change your life". This is just one example of how to emphasize certain words to make different statements.

22) "I wonder if you will.....*just forget you had a problem*".

An example of a simple direct suggestion.

23) *"Now*...let.........*your unconscious now....take care of you for a change....*

Here is a good example of suggestion being tied into the previous sentence to make a command statement. As in the item 22 above: "Just forget you had a problem......now...... becomes the statement "Just forget you had the problem now." This brings it into the present and gives instruction. As the suggestion continues the statement instructs "your unconscious...now..." Once again this implies the patient/client is unconscious now. It continues on another deeper level implying that the unconscious will take care of them for a change". What change? The change they are looking for, of course!

24) *"Drift   deeper.....into   deeper states..........of......relaxxxxxxxxxxx.....ation"*

Direct suggestion to drift and deepen then stress and elongate the word relax (as a command) adding the suffix " ation" after a short delay. This adds some confusion and the subconscious knows this as a command to relax.

25) *"Now.....*I know you are wondering how......to ......*make sense of all this"*

The word "now" adds to the previous commands in item 24. Speak this in downward inflection after a short delay. Then, at the end of the sentence using downward inflection again, give the embedded command to "make sense of all this".

26) "Wonder leads to learning and since.......*your unconscious.......now.......*"

Another embedded command, very powerful once mastered.

27) "You can......*learn all you need for a change*"

A final embedded command to "learn all you need...for a change"!

Now you can practice any and all the above sentence structures to use in conversation or formal induction. Another great way to utilize the above suggestions is to combine them to make a complete induction and suggestive therapeutic exchange! Below you can find the example I use to effect change in patients/clients:

Using Language to Effect Change

➤ So it is OK to... *relax now*...or in a minute....it doesn't really matter

➤ When you....*go into trance*

➤ It can, you know, be *easy to let go*...

➤ To let ...*your unconscious*....mind help you

➤ *Resolve your issues now*

➤ So....as you *drift and relax*

➤ You may be aware of sensations in your body....as you ....*Relax more.*

➤ You know....a person is able to...*develop an internal focus of attention*

➤ And just... *feel good* about themselves....

➤ And...eventually that troublesome issue will just

disappear.

➤ Isn't it nice to know

➤ You can...*integrate these learnings*

➤ Whenever...*your unconscious*...is ready

➤ It is enjoyable to *learn something new*...isn't it?

➤ A person might...you know...get a whole new perspective

➤ When you allow *your unconscious*...generate new solutions.

➤ I wonder if you have already started to notice

➤ *Changes taking place...*

➤ When you really begin to... *make these patterns a part of your life*

➤ Then...you'll *free yourself to change*

➤ By the time you.....*Notice how far you have come......*

➤ You can be excited about the positive change in your life

41

> I wonder if you will.....*just forget you had a problem*

> *Now*...let.........*your unconscious now....take care of you for a change....*

> *Drift   deeper.....into   deeper states..........of......relaxxxxxxxxxxx.....ation*

> *Now*.....I know you are wondering how......to ......*make sense of all this*

> Wonder leads to learning and since.......*your unconscious......now......*

> You can......*learn all you need for a change*

You should now begin to notice how stressing certain words, emphasizing others, using appropriate deliberate pauses when speaking can lead to very effective suggestion delivery. Hypnotic interventions are after all, suggestion driven for the most part, so learning to deliver effective suggestions is important.

Agreement

Salespeople have used agreement for years to help close sales. If the salesperson states three things that are true, a person is more likely to agree with the fourth as being true as well. This is sometimes known as the "Yes Set". Establishing an agreement pattern with your patient/client is easy to do simply stating the obvious so they realize what you are saying is true.

"You are sitting there in that chair…..breathing in and out……listening to my words…….you can relax more now….."

The above structure is done in an indirect style with the words "you can relax more now". There is no direct command "relax now" but that could be inserted here as well depending on the rapport and the patient you have in the chair. The words "you can relax more now" allows more the possibility of agreement as it is somewhat less threatening to some individuals. This is in fact what I call a "possibility" question or command. These type of questions offer possibilities that would be difficult to refute. Some examples:

"Can you begin to hope for something amazing to happen...."?

"Can you aspire to greater happiness and health..."?

"Can you imagine becoming more adept at suggestion delivery..."?

These questions are all answered in the affirmative by most individuals. They are a super method to begin an agreement set. Another type of suggestion to use to develop agreement is a reality statement question. Examples like:

"Isn't it a bonus to get more than your money's worth"?

"Isn't it great to have the money you need to do what you want"?

"Is it true that people have survived great tribulations in the past"?

These are all answered in the positive and can develop the agreement set quickly. Now we can add to the above by encouraging the imagination.

"Would you know when you have gotten more than your money's worth"? Most people would agree quickly with that question.

"Would it be possible for people to endure great tribulations in the future"? Yes of course!

You can begin to see how combining these questions in several different ways can lead to a powerful development of an agreement set. Once this is done the individual is more likely to follow subsequent suggestions. They become more accustomed to the affirmative mindset rather than a negative mindset. This is similar to what lawyers will do in the courtroom, asking questions that will be answered in the affirmative and then interjecting (for an example), "Did you kill that man?", hoping for an affirmative answer.

Presuppositions

The presupposition is not a direct statement, instead, the meaning is assumed in the delivery of the suggestion itself. Words that presuppose something will happen, lead to this assumption.

Spontaneously, automatically, readily, unconsciously, constantly, intermittently...

Example: *"As you relax you* **automatically** *go deeper,* **unconsciously** *processing the information...."*

As you can see some of these words are time orientation, some are descriptive and so forth. They lend to the assumption that something will happen or has already occurred.

These words presuppose something is true:

Actually, genuinely, definitely, undeniably, etc.

Example: *"All that really matters.... is that you* **actually** *relax more now...."*

With just using the above two patterns you can make very

persuasive suggestions to your client/patients.

Example: "You can begin to feel those relaxing feelings *intermittently* at first, then *constantly* and *actually* you may discover that *undeniably* you *feel better now*...."

Binds

It is interesting to note that the use of presuppositions is a major part of using a bind.

Binds are questions asked of a patient/client that they answer consciously. One of the most often used binds is the question: "Do you want to go into trance in that chair or in the hypnosis chair over there"? When answering the question the decision by the client binds the client into going into trance no matter which is chosen? This type of bind is most often used during trance induction.

Double binds are very persuasive and one of the most effective indirect suggestive techniques. They can be used to induce trance and /or effect change. The double bind gives the patient/client a choice; however that choice is really only an illusion! When the patient/client is asked to make choice between to alternatives, it is already presupposed that the behavior suggested will occur. Example: "Do you want a Pepsi or Coke"? This already presupposes they are going to drink a cola. The patient/client answers without being aware they have committed to the behavior already.

Double binds are an unconsciously answered query. An example: "Are you becoming more relaxed when you exhale or when you inhale"? The presupposition is the patient is already in the relaxed state and requires them to go inward and wait for that relaxed state in order to answer. This process is assistive in getting patients to relax or go into trance or, other.

You can enhance the use of binds even more to add to the dissociation occurring in trance. A conscious/unconscious double bind is very similar to a double bind but they emphasize the conscious - unconscious dissociation. An example: "Your conscious mind can remember memories of fun vacation times while your unconscious...can recall other times, I wonder which happens first"? This type of double bind requires the individual to wait for an answer at an unconscious level and also emphasize to themselves the differences between conscious and unconscious. These types of conscious/unconscious double binds are extremely effective in adding to dissociation and helping to eliminate interference from conscious awareness during therapy. This method of illusory choice bypasses the conscious mind and the resulting subconscious agreement sets up an effective result.

Patient/Client Interpretations of Self

Patients will present with predetermined interpretations of both objective and subjective data. This information may be factual or fantasy. It has been said by Stephen Brooks (personal communication, 2011), that the fantasy portion of their information is subjective and because patients/clients are so bound up within their particular problem they present with large amounts of information based on their subjective interpretations. Because these interpretations are subjective they may not be based in real fact and thus are not useful to the therapist. Many professionals doing therapy get caught up in attempting to understand these subjective beliefs and/or believing them and begin to go down a very long procedural path.

Since many presenting problems involve other people, patients also bring a large amount of information based on their subjective interpretations of other people's behavior. Mind reading on the part of the patient muddies the therapeutic water and is usually not based in fact. As a therapist you should acknowledge these interpretations, BUT maintain relevance otherwise the therapist as well as the patient gets lost in the ensuing confusion. Many times the patient has attempted to self-diagnose and in doing so reads tremendous amounts of pop psychology journals and/or other information available to the populace. This information can confuse a plan of care especially if this subjective interpretation is based upon popular psychological reference that appears to be plausible.

Some Examples

"Everyone in my family has migraine headaches".

"It's in my genes..."

"She/he should not behave like that..."

"I must have had problems in a past life and now this..."

What to do

You must always maintain relevance. Professionals must intervene and challenge these subjective interpretations otherwise the patient/client may continue on ad-nauseum. You can interject the statement: "Yes but how *is that relevant* to this problem now?" Do this in a non-blaming way so there is no possibility of damaging rapport or misinterpretation that you are somehow ridiculing the patient. Once attention is brought to the subjective interpretations you can then redirect to a more realistic factually based assessment of the problem. Surely make note of the patients ideas and let them know that you may refer to them in a future session but continue to maintain relevance constantly. Stay on track and refocus the patient/client.

Examples

"That is interesting, but how can you be sure?"

"Thank you for that information but how do you see (feel, hear) that as relevant?"

"You may be right or you may be wrong in this, right now we cannot be sure so we can table those thoughts for a while"…"

"Yes I can see, (hear, feel) that right now, but how realistic is that?"

You can also ask the patient/client to repeat their interpretation several times as if you did not quite "get it". This may allow the patient time to consciously become aware of incorrect interpretations when reciting them over and over out loud. Once you become accustomed to working this way it becomes easier to accomplish the goal of maintaining relevance, Always "reeling" in the patient to factual objective data. It is important to stick with the facts and not let their imagination begin to answer.

Using Language

Once again let us take a look at how to put language and style to work to deliver effective suggestive therapy. Let me give you several examples of language and style that will assist the patient/client to "go inside" and focus there awareness. I will use the words and phrases: "notice", "Have you ever..", Focus your awareness on...", and ".....which means....."

Notice

Let's begin with the word "Notice". This word commands attention and the patient/client will often begin to "look for" or "attend to" what you the therapist is stating.

1) *"Notice* how comfortable you can become with each breath in and out"

2) *"Begin to notice* the changes already taking place within...."

3) *"You may already have noticed* how good you can feel doing this..."

Using the phrases and words above in your suggestive therapy will assist you in becoming more familiar with working hypnotically in your practice. In the above you begin to identify that changing verb tense is and can be, very powerful in suggestive therapeutics. Past and past perfect verb tense begins to put problems into the past for patients and clients and can in fact, be the seminal step in helping them to recover and/or change.

Focus Your Awareness

This phrase begins to direct the client/patient to begin to do something.

1) "Focus your awareness on your left foot and begin to notice how comfortable you begin to feel"

2) "Now that you have focused your attention on your breathing...."

3) "Once you begin to focus on the picture, you can begin to notice how...."

Using this one phrase, for example, you can put together an effective paragraph of suggestion that moves the clients awareness from place to place and time frame to time frame.

"It is interesting to discover that once you focus on your left foot, you begin to notice how comfortable your breathing has become. Focusing on your comfort level has enabled you to become aware of an increasing level of relaxation...."

Have You Ever

This phrase engages the memories of the patient/client. It is a very easy method to begin having a patient regress. After all, every time we access a memory we are, in fact, doing an age regression.

1) "Have you ever looked at clouds passing by in the sky?"

2) "Have you ever wondered what it will be like when you enter trance?"

3) "Have you ever noticed how good you felt when you awaken from certain dreams?

From the above you can begin to assemble several effective phrase patterns that will enable you to become more effective. "I have often looked at clouds passing in the sky, I wonder, have you ever looked at clouds passing by in the sky?"

Which Means

Now we can add a linkage phrase. This will enable you to link words and phrases in a manner that seems very logical to the patient/client hearing the phrase.

1) "You are sitting in the chair and breathing in and out, *which means* you can begin to relax more..."

2) "Reading these words now *means that* you are able to process information at an unconscious level and *that means* you will soon be incorporating these phrases in your work"

3) "You are reading this text on Doing Hypnosis *which means,* you have an interest in using these phrases in your work...."

Ambiguities

Ambiguities are really neat tools to deliver suggestion unconsciously. When inserting them into sentence structure they can many times appear strange, yet, the unconscious processes the command. This type of delivery requires words that can be used as both noun and verb. When inserting that particular word make the remaining words that follow be the command. Then continue with the original topic line.

Example:

" and is it not interesting to note that all this can **benefit** *by making this change now*.....because you are applying new knowledge..."

Or

"reading this book helps you to **focus** *all your abilities to make the change* and you will begin to understand more of....."

Or

" these learnings can **direct** *your thoughts to make the change* now……"

Or

" you will be able to do things easier and more effortless when you **work** *this into your subconscious* from now onward and……

Many of these types of words are available:

Fix, mend, send, tie, sew, load, mail, box, pack, place, and many more. These can all be used as an ambiguity (noun/verb) in a sentence or conversation. These then become powerful suggestions that are overlooked by the conscious awareness yet are acted upon by the subconscious mind.

By now you have begun to discover the power in using language patterns. These patterns can be used alone or together to effect positive outcomes in your patient/client. Another example of a powerful type of language pattern is the use of distracting sentences. These are sentences completely out of context place within a conversation. The out of context sentence requires the listener to focus inward (go into trance) to discover the possible meaning of the sentence. This sentence is then followed immediately by an embedded command that is completely ignored by the conscious mind of the listener.

Example:

"I have had many patients in to stop smoking. Many patients stopped immediately and some took several days or a week. *My brother believes dogs can fly. So sit down and relax now* in that hypnosis chair and....."

The command suggestion "...so sit down and relax now" follows the out of context sentence "My brother believes dogs can fly". As the individual concentrates their focus inward to create some meaning, the suggestions are then sent directly to the unconscious mind.

Putting It All Together

Practicing the above materials will enable you to become effective at delivering suggestion in your practice. The following several "Problems" are very common and I will model a therapeutic suggestion session.

Stress

Stress is an everyday occurrence. Managing stress is an everyday problem for many people. Here is an example of using this type of language and style to begin to effect change for your client. See if you can identify the different items I incorporate into this easy to learn suggestive theme.

"So it is OK to… *relax now*…or in a minute….it doesn't really matter

When you….*go into trance*

It can, you know, be *easy to let go*…

To let …*your unconscious*….mind help you

61

Resolve your issues now

So....as you *drift and relax*

You may be aware of sensations in your body....as you

....*Relax more.*

You know....a person is able to...*develop an internal focus*

of attention

And just... *feel good* about themselves....

And...eventually that troublesome issue will just disappear.

Isn't it nice to know

You can...*integrate these learnings*

Whenever...*your unconscious*...is ready

It is enjoyable to *learn something new*...isn't it?

A person might...you know...get a whole new perspective

When you allow *your unconscious*...generate new solutions.

I wonder if you have already started to notice

Changes taking place...

When you really begin to... *make these patterns a part of*

your life

Then…you'll *free yourself to change*

By the time you…..*Notice how far you have come……*

You can be excited about the positive change in your life

I wonder if you will…..*just forget you had a problem*

Now…let………your unconscious now….take care of you for

a change….

Drift deeper…..into deeper

states………of……relaxxxxxxxxxxx…..ation

*Now…..*I know you are wondering how……to ……*make*

sense of all this

Wonder leads to learning and since…….*your*

unconscious……now……

You can……*learn all you need for a change*

OR

I wonder if….you ***focus your awareness*** on your left ear lobe

You can notice the differences in your left foot…..

Which means.........that **discomfort has already begun to change**....as you **relax more deeply now**........

Have you ever....found you had gotten a paper cut and not known when it happened?

Some people..... never...... **notice the anesthesia for that discomfort** when it happens....

Which means they......... **never feel it**......

You can begin to discover from the above two short examples how to begin to incorporate these suggestions for your patients/clients. Add a presupposition and it looks like this:

" *Which means* ....**unconsciously**.....that,....

discomfort has already begun to change..."

The proper use of inflection, pause, embedded commands and the use of presuppositions and other techniques as already discussed provide a very powerful method of delivering suggestions!

References

Bandler, R (2008). *Richard Bandler's guide to trance-formation.* Deerfeild Beach Florida: Health Communications Inc.

Battino, R. (2007). Expectation: Principles and practice of very brief therapy. *Contemporary Hypnosis 24*(1), 19-29.

Birdwhistle, R., L. (1970). *Kinesics and context: Essays on body-motion communication.* University of Pennsylvania Press.

Brown, A., and Draper, F. (2003). Accommodative speech and terms of endearment, elements of language mode often experienced by older adults. *Journal of Advanced Nursing, 41*(1), 15-21.

Brown, P. (1991). *The hypnotic brain.* New Haven, CT: Yale University Press

Crist, J., Armer, J., & Radina, M. (2002). A study in cultural diversity: Caregiving for the old order Amish elder with Alzheimer's disease. *Journal of Multicultural Nursing & Health 8* (3). 78-85.

Coll, A., Ameen, J., & Mead, D. (2004). Postoperative pain assessment tools in day surgery: Literature review. *Journal of Advanced Nursing 46*(2), 124-133.

Comer, R. J. (2001). *Abnormal psychology 4th ed.* New York: Worth Publishers.

Estabrooks, G. (1957). *Hypnotism.*

Hilgard, E. R. (1965). *Hypnotic susceptibility.* New York: Harcourt, Brace, & Jovanavich.

Hilgard, E. R., & Hilgard, J. R., (1994). *Hypnosis in the relief of pain.* (Rev. ed.) New York: Brunner/Mazel.

Holden, C. (1988). Effects of relaxation with guided imagery on surgical stress and wound healing. *Research in Nursing & Health, 11,* 235-244.

Jensen, M. (2011). *Hypnosis for chronic pain management: Therapists guide.* New York, New York, Oxford University Press.

Kane, S. & Olness, K. (2004). *The art of therapeutic communication: The collected works of Kay F. Thompson.* Carmarthen UK: Crown House Publishers.

Kozier, B., Erb, G., Berman, A., & Snyder, S. (2004). *Fundamentals of nursing: Concepts, process and practice (7ᵗʰ ed.).* Upper Saddle River, NJ: Prentice-Hall.

Mackey, C. (2005). Complementary & Alternative Therapies in *Faith Community Nursing. Pp . 193-209.* Philadelphia, PA: Lippincott William & Wilkens.

Mackey, C. (2005). Acute Spinal Cord Injury in *Manual of Critical Care Nursing 5ᵗʰ Ed. Pp.* 136-149. Philadelphia, PA

Mackey, E. F. (2010). Effects of hypnosis as an adjunct to intravenous sedation for third molar extraction: A randomized, blind, controlled study. *The Interantional Journal of Clinical and Experimental Hypnosis 58*(1): 21-38.

Mackey, E. F. (2009). Age regression: A case study. *Annals of the American Psychotherapy Association 12*(4) 46-49.

Mehrabian, A. & Ferris, S. (1967). Inference of attitudes from non-verbal communication in two channels. *Journal of Consulting Psychology, 3:* 248-252.

Roykulcharoen, V. & Good, M. (2004). Systematic relaxation to relieve postoperative pain. *Journal of Advanced Nursing, 48*(2), 140-148.

Voit, R., & Delaney, M. (2004). Hypnosis in clinical practice: Steps for mastering hypnotherapy. New York: Brunner-Routledge.

White, P. (2004). We are what we say. *Nursing Standard 25,*

(18) 88.

Yapko, M. (2003). Trancework: An introduction to the

practice of clinical hypnosis 3rd ed. New York:

Brunner-Routledge.

Santrock, J. (2006). *Life Span Development* (10th ed.).

Boston, MA: McGraw-Hill.

Made in the USA
Monee, IL
23 November 2020

49174844R10039